OI[illegible] FIRE[illegible]ERS

by Sunita Apte

Harcourt
SCHOOL PUBLISHERS

Cover, ©Explorer/Photo Researchers, Inc.; p.4, ©AP Photo/Yahya Ahmed; p.5, ©Steve McCurry/ Magnum Photos; p.6, ©AP Photo/Yahya Ahmed; p.7, ©Lowell Georgia/CORBIS; p.8, ©Anders Pettersson/Getty Images; p.9, ©Anders Pettersson/Getty Images; p.10, ©Paul Schutzer/Time Life Pictures/Getty Images; p.11, ©UNIVERSAL/THE KOBAL COLLECTION; p.12, ©Steve McCurry/ Magnum Photos; p.13, ©Robert van der Hilst/CORBIS; p.14, ©AFP PHOTO/FILE/PASCAL GUYOT/ Getty Images.

Printed in the United States of America

ISBN 10: 0-15-350576-1
ISBN 13: 978-0-15-350576-8

Ordering Options
ISBN 10: 0-15-350336-X (Grade 6 Below-Level Collection)
ISBN 13: 978-0-15-350336-8 (Grade 6 Below-Level Collection)
ISBN 10: 0-15-357583-2 (package of 5)
ISBN 13: 978-0-15-357583-9 (package of 5)

1 2 3 4 5 6 7 8 9 10 179 12 11 10 09 08 07 06

An oil well is on fire. The flames shoot up hundreds of feet into the air. Thick black smoke fills the sky. Let's find out more about oil wells.

Oil wells are created by drilling holes into the earth in oil-rich areas. Most oil wells have many millions of gallons of oil, which burns easily. The fire could burn until every drop of that oil is gone. The longer the fire goes, the worse things get. The fire is bad for the environment. It makes the air unsafe for people who live nearby. The company that owns the oil well loses money. The oil that the company wants to sell is burning up.

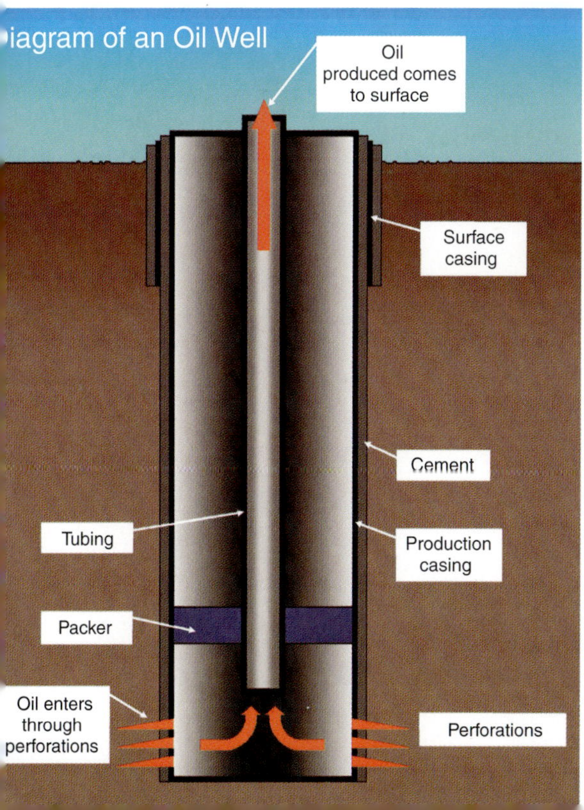

The fire must be stopped, but how? Who is equipped to do such dangerous and filthy work?

Oil well firefighters can do the job. They are specially trained firefighters who put out fires in oil wells.

These firefighters do important work. They travel all over the world putting out oil well fires. Each time they fight a fire, they risk their lives. They have to do dangerous things and use very dangerous materials to get the job done.

Oil well fires are different from other kinds of fires. They can burn for months or even years before being put out. Unlike most forest fires, for example, oil well fires don't spread. Only the oil in the well itself burns.

The dangers in fighting the fire come from exposure to the smoke and the heat from the fire. The temperature inside the burning well can be over 1,000° Fahrenheit (538°C). Many oil wells are in the desert. Fires in these desert wells can be hot enough to melt the desert sand, turning it into glass!

The first trick for oil well firefighters is getting near such a hot fire. Before tackling a big oil well fire, the firefighters will often dig a giant hole and fill it with water that comes from a natural water supply like a river. They might dig a reserve hole as well. Then they will use hoses and trucks to spray the water from these holes onto the fire. This cools down the area enough to allow the firefighters to get near. Still, the firefighters often have to use tin shelters to protect themselves from the heat and fumes near the well.

When water alone is not enough to put out an oil well fire, more extreme measures must be taken. The firefighters have to bring out dynamite to do the job.

Oil well firefighters sometimes use dynamite to create an explosion in the oil well. They will need lots and lots of dynamite. They might need more than 200 pounds (91 kg) of it.

The explosion eats up all the oxygen around the well. A fire relies on oxygen to burn. Without the oxygen, the oil well fire goes out.

However, in some ways, putting out the fire is the easy part. Once the fire is finally out, the really dangerous work begins.

The firefighters must cap the well to stop the flow of oil. That way, the fire can't start again.

Capping a well after a fire is the most dangerous part of oil well firefighting. Though the fire is out, plenty of oil fumes still linger in the air. These fumes are extremely flammable. One spark and the whole area could go up in flames again. In fact, the second fire could be even worse than the first!

The wells are capped very carefully by teams of firefighters. A paramedic is usually part of the team. This way, if firefighters get hurt, they can get medical attention immediately.

The firefighters who cap the wells are known as "blowout specialists." Sometimes, the blowout specialists are hampered by giant puddles of oil and chemicals near the well. They have to wade through the puddles. To protect themselves, they wear two sets of clothing. Still, their skin gets covered in oil by the end of the day.

Red Adair

Red Adair was perhaps the most famous oil well firefighter of all. His real name was Paul Neal Adair, but he was called Red because of his bright red hair. He began fighting oil fires after serving in the army during World War II.

Red became famous in 1962. That's when he put out a natural gas fire in the Sahara Desert. The fire had burned for six months before Red was hired to put it out.

Flames from the fire shot over 400 feet (122 m) into the air. That's a lot of altitude! The fire was so big that astronauts could see it from space. It was so hot that the desert sand around it had melted into glass.

Red created an explosion in the gas well. That put the fire out. Then he capped the well. People all over the world heard about what he had done.

In 1968, Hollywood made a movie based on Red's life. The famous actor John Wayne played an oil well firefighter like Red. Red served as an advisor on the movie. By then, he was already the most famous oil well firefighter in the world.

John Wayne playing an oil well firefighter

In 1991, Red Adair and a number of other oil well firefighters faced a challenge that overshadowed any oil well fire that they had ever had to fight before. In the Middle East nation of Kuwait, 650–750 oil wells were on fire. After the end of the Gulf War, the defeated country set fire to all of Kuwait's oil wells. The smoke from them blackened the sky over the whole country.

Oil companies were worried about losing lots of money. Others were worried about pollution from the smoke. Everyone knew the fires had to be put out as quickly as possible.

The world's best oil well firefighters rushed to Kuwait. There, they worked day and night to put out the fires. The work was difficult, dangerous, and exhausting.

People said it would take years to put out all the oil well fires. They were wrong. Red and the others had all the fires put out in six months. That meant the oil companies could begin to pump oil again. It also meant the skies in Kuwait cleared up. Everyone was happy. Red was once again hailed as a hero.

As long as there are oil wells, there will always be oil well firefighters. The work they do is extremely dangerous and dirty. However, it's also very rewarding. Oil well fires can be tricky. Figuring out how to put one out can be a real challenge.

It's a challenge oil well firefighters enjoy. Many of them travel far from home, sometimes for months at a time. Sometimes they get injured. Often they get completely covered in oil. Most of them, though, wouldn't think of doing anything else. When a big oil well fire erupts, they wouldn't miss it for the world.

Think Critically

1. What is the main idea of this book?
2. Who is considered the world's most famous oil well firefighter? How did he become famous?
3. What are the two steps to putting out an oil well fire?
4. How does the author feel about oil well firefighters? How can you tell?
5. Would you ever consider becoming an oil well firefighter? Why or why not?

Science

Ignition Temperatures Use the internet or other library resources to find the temperature at which oil starts to burn. Find the ignition temperature of three other materials (for example, wood, gasoline, and steel). Make a bar graph comparing these temperatures.

School-Home Connection Discuss oil well fires with an adult at home. Talk about why oil well fires are dangerous not just for firefighters but for the communities nearby as well.

Word Count: 1,165 (with graphic 1,187)